The Dream of the Rood
(A Prose Version)

Gregg Glory
(Gregg G. Brown)

BLAST PRESS
324B Matawan Ave
Cliffwood, NJ 07721
amazon.com/author/gregglory
gregglory at aol.com

Contents

Caedmon's Hymn　　4

The Dream of the Rood　　9

About the Translator　　26

Caedmon's Hymn

Now singeth pitched praise
            of high-heaven's Warden,
Mightiest Maker
           and his masterful mind-plans!
Works of the Wonder-Father
           who established each wonder
(Dear eternal Lord)
           and their foundations fathomed.

He earliest scraped,
      for all mankind's sons,
The sky's heaven-roof,
       O holy Creator;
Then made He middle-earth,
      this mankind-Warden,
Eternal Lord;
     and afterwards fashioned
Firm earth-folds for us,
      our Almighty Master.

As I walked through the wilderness of this world, I lighted on a certain place where there was a Den, and I laid me down in that place to sleep; and, as I slept, I dreamed a dream. I dreamed, and behold I saw a man clothed with rags, standing at a certain place, with his face from his own house, a book in his hand, and a great burden upon his back (Isaiah lxiv.6; Luke xiv.33; Psalms xxxvii.4; Habakkuk ii.2; Acts xvi.31). I looked and saw him open the book and read therein; and, as he read, he wept, and trembled; and not being able any longer to contain himself, he brake out with a lamentable cry, saying, "What shall I do?" (Acts 11.37).

—John Bunyan, *The Pilgrim's Progress*

The Dream of the Rood

(A Prose Version)

Listen sweetly, for I will tell a dream—of all dreams, the best—come to me at guilty midnight, while the other voices slept, and I was wakeful.

Before me twisted and rose up a wondrous Rood, brighter than leaf-light, enveloped by beams.

Burnished as a battle-standard, it stood, lovingly covered in gilt foil of gold.

Where its root-end reached earth lay bright tangles of rivery gems; five gems as big as knuckles shone at the cross' crux, bound tight as a dovetail joint.

Fair-formed hosts of eternal angels gazed glowingly down upon this gorgeous cross; certainly, this was no sinner's gallows, framed for felons.

Holy spirits beheld it there, and all good men upon the earth earnestly stared, and all of God's glorious creation circled round and cradled the wondrous Rood in its heart.

Splendid indeed rose the triumph-tree!

And I, sin-stained, a worm sore-wounded, full of faults and afeared, looked and saw the very cross of glory. Resplendently robed was the tree, shining in joy, adored and adorned in rich gold.

Gems, too numerous to count, covered the Lord's tree like Christmas tinsel, shedding splendor in the air.

Even so, in my quiet depth of deep-night thought, through the sharp gems and glimmering curtains of wave-wrought gold, my mind perceived the old animosity of ancient evil-doers still lingering.

Indeed, I saw, on the tree's right side, blood had begun to slowly flow.

And I, all grievy with sorrow, and troubled, and afraid, my knees weak and backward as a bird's, felt the fear of my smallness before such a beautiful sight.

The wonderful Rood flickered before me; sometimes dark with heavy fluids, moist to the touch, soaked to the core with dread blood; sometimes frosted with layers of gilded treasure.

A long time I lay there, watching the tree flicker between being wounded and wealth-ridden; a long time, with my troubles upon me, and unacknowledged tears slowing flowing from my open, yet dreaming, eyes.

And then, I heard the Rood speak. This exalted and excellent tree spoke aloud these words:

"Although it happened eons ago, still I recall all, and remember brightly, the day I was cut down at the dark wood's edge....

My roots ripsawed from beneath me, my foundations foundered.

My sweet wood was broken by strong men, bent to their bending, then bound, hammered and hefted up: a cross— crafted to crucify criminals.

I, who ought to have been a shapely harp or been soothingly tooled to sing out soft songs at a summer fair, myself a fair-fashioned flute!

Hard those hands upon me, their palms unpleasant, rough-ready, raw.

Hoisted, tossed on the enemy's shoulders, high we crested the cold hill where they planted me, placed torn root to turned soil; ungrowing, I rested as an ill man rests: feverish, distressed.

Then came the Lord. Not weary, His aspect. Not trodden-down, not bested.

Then cameth the Lord, bright-breasted, restless. With zeal He sprang up the hill, sprinting to mount me. As a knight surmounts his horse at battle-day dawn, thus bravely He came.

As a woman, worried in winter, the earth trembled. And lo, I trembled, as before the ax had bitten my haft. But I dare not bow down beneath my burden, nor burst like a rotted tree unshipworthy at sea.

His battle-standard and steed, I stood, firm from wronged roots to man-handled cross-arms. Firm, aye, though I quailed within.

Then the young hero stepped simply from his robe, stripped to nakedness before His enemies' eyes (that was God Almighty standing there).

With easy strength and resolute look, He ascended.

Now upon the gallows was the Christ-King, brave before badness, and seen by all so that he might redeem them once and forever.

I dare not bow to earth with my burden; though he embraced me, and I trembled.

Now was I a risen cross, lifting the King of Kings, Lord of Heaven and of us, a man bruised and humbled.

Now I dare not bow down with my burden; though I embraced Him, and He trembled.

With black nails they pierced us! On me, still, are the scars. Look and see. Behold them, bloody and open, wronging wounds of malice and menace.

Merrily, they mocked us, us both together; crowing, crowded rowdily below us.

Together were we tied; together troubled with toilsome blood, still leaking from the man's side after His spirit had departed, flown away, returned to His Father in heaven.

Woeful fate! To endure, as I have endured, all that happened there—cruelly occured on the bare earthen mount.

I had felt the Lord of the heavenly hosts severely stretched against my grain.

Darkness came, covering with modest clouds low-hung the bright dignity of that good man's corpse. A shadow went forth upon the plains surrounding, and darkness was on all the land and sky.

All creation was weeping, wracked to know our dear King's death.

Christ was still upon the cross; his body broken, crownless and crushed.

Natheless, from afar off came many men and women eager to view the pierced Prince.

All this I beheld, bound to the Lord.

Sorrow, sorrow was great upon me; within me grievous gnashings and sadness.

Now I bowed again to the eager hands of many men; humbly bowed, happily bent down.

With faithful fervor they unbound the broken man, lifted Him like a warrior from the field; with friendly hands and with brothers' tears they bore Him from His terrible torment.

Abandoned I stood, drenched in dewy blood; straight nails stood out from my skin like arrows, and my wounds knew no rest.

Gently, gently they lay Him down. Gently laid out His weary limbs, and washed they Him.

Stood they all around His head as a human crown, gazing awhile at the silent savior, weary-limbed after His long battle.

Dug they then in the clay-cast cracks of the rock, scraping sepulcher in sight of His slayers. Stone-flakes brimmed the hard earth-bank, brightened the drab dank.

At sunset they bore Him in, the Lord of Victories into the cave's clasp taken.

Misericordia they sang, all wretched together at the cave-mouth, in the early time of evening. At length, they all left, singly and in pairs, harrow-hearted over the earth, leaving their uncompanioned Prince little company.

We three crosses stood there a long time, from our burdens unbound, weeping blood as the congregation of stars came singly in sight, and the warrior-voices faded far over the faint grey hill.

The body within the tomb grew cool, pleasant abode of the absent spirit.

Other men returned, ragged and chained, and buried us pit-deep in the dirt ordained for our grave-holes. Dreadful, woeful, our second hewing! Dark was our dirt house.

There was I found, by the Lord's friends' fingers discovered; they lifted me up and adorned me as with silver samite, enwrapped me with gold foil and precious gems.

You, who dream this, hear all the evils I have endured for the Lord, endless grief experienced, pain and terror gathered close in one place.

And now, by time transformed, from that nadir I am come to glory, and men all over the face of creation honour me in every fashion, praying penitent at the sign of the cross.

In my two arms, God's sole Son suffered for some pitiful while.

Thereby do I now tower tall under glorious heaven! Rise I up, empowered to bring balm to all who deem me blessed, and who in awe do homage to Him I held.

I, who had been since the before-times a torture-tree, terrible and hated, am become blessed. Through me the path, the truth, liveth and beginneth for every seeker after the way.

Most blessed of all trees I became, who had been most despised and spat upon.

The Prince of All, and the high Kingdom's mighty Master, blessed me in this as He had blessed His mother Mary, of all women the worthiest.

Take now this tale of trial, this tribulation deliver from thy sleep, for it is wholesome, a holy vision vouchsafed to thee, my beloved dreamer.

Say well these words; with weariless voice proclaim them, and with praise sustain thy saying: Upon this glorious tree, Almighty God Himself suffered trouble and torture for mankind's sins' sake, and the ancient deeds of Old Adam.

Here tasted He bitter death. Died He upon me.

Oh, the Lord arose then, puissant in prowess as a lion, rising to take weak humanity's hand, to guide the guileless and grieve the guilty.

To heaven He hastened, departing far hence, past the sun's blazing bauble.

Great God, creation's Maker, Lord of All the heavenly host, most wise, waits above to visit His minions again, to teach mankind on the Day of Judgment.

Angels in his vanguard, He shall ride down upon us, shall voice His virtuous verdict on that last day, shall deal unto each soul its earned deserts, wages won during life's vivid brevity.

None on that day shall stand without fear of His justice, but all shall tremble mightily in the sight of the Lord and fear His word.

He will turn to His blessed angels and ask the beauteous multitude:

'Where is the man who will die the death, bitterly wracked, for my sake? Where is the man who will die for me, as I have died for him upon the victory-tree?'

Then those who have given their fate no forethought, and lived vain and wasteful lives, will shiver verily, and their livers blanche with cold cowardice.

For what can they say to Christ? What plea prepare on their own behalf?

Yet none need be afeared who fare forth with my best token upon his breast, or beating within it.

Through the cross come all to Christ. Here pass all paths of those who sojourn toward Heaven, directing their feet to follow that suffering man, He who goes before and prepareth a place.

There, indeed, shall be an abiding Kingdom for each soul who walks this wrathful world and wisheth to dwell with the Lord."

Fervently I prayed then to the Rood, zestful in zeal, in spirit blithe, although I abideth alone in my room.

Now my spirit roused me, ravished me, rousted me, bade me race onward to my urgent task.

Full many a lonely hour had I lived before, languishing lone in my small solitude.

But now my life's mission is made anew; hope stings me on to seek out that triumphant tree my vision vouchsafed.

Patient as a pilgrim I pursue my dream's demand, in adoring duty I press forward so that all souls may find faith through Christ's cross. Hear me, and hope!

Few friends have I here, among the Earth's mighty men. Long since have they left daylight's delight, the company of cousins, and all the world's welter of joys.

Sought they by dying the King of Glory; departed, they now reside in resplendent

Heaven, abiding beside God, alight in His splendour.

Dwell they now in deathless glory, while I alone greet each day longing for the Rood's return. My imperishable wish is to see the Rood again as I had seen it in my dream.

My dream was goodly, God-begotten its origins, though I go sin-wounded and lost through this woeful world.

Fetch me up, good Cross, to where God's great bliss forever is; and bear me hence to that place of gladness.

There sit the people of Heaven, and the Eternal Lord also beside them, seated at that bountiful feast, and singing betimes, beautiful to behold and gracious in all manner of things.

Establish me among that heavenly throng, holy Cross; set me down amidst the saints and pour me wine and let us delight together in that ever-living splendor.

May the Lord be my friend, I pray, who suffered Sin on Earth for our sake, redeeming mankind upon the tree.

Hotly He harrowed Hell, after rising, bringing blessings and bliss to those souls enduring fierce fires below the Earth. The Son in His solitude strode hellward, flying homeward triumphant—strong and sure He returned.

With singular *geste* He led the myriad damned back to the His Kingdom's abiding bliss, where in high Heaven they live glad days with all of the saints and the heavenly hosts of Angels.

Thus it was in joyous company that our divine Ruler, the good Lord God Himself, came home again.

finis

About the Translator

Gregg Glory (Gregg G. Brown) has devoted his life to poetry since happening across a haiku by Moritake, to wit:

> Leaves
>
> float back up to the branch—
>
> Ah! butterflies.

He runs the micro-publishing house BLAST PRESS, which has published over two dozen authors in the past 25 years. Named in honor of the wild Vorticist venture by Ezra Pound and Wyndham Lewis, BLAST PRESS is forward-looking and very opinionated.

He still composes poems on his departed father's clipboard, which he's had since High School.

He wishes all of his family and friends

A Very Merry Christmas!

2012

Printed in Great Britain
by Amazon